Questions

Intermediate
Differentiated Curriculum

Grade Levels
4th – 6th

Length of Time
40+ hours

ISBN 978-1-59363-288-5
© 2008 Prufrock Press Inc.

1

Prufrock Press' Differentiated Curriculum Kits provide hands-on, discovery-based, research-oriented activities that are cross-curricular. Prufrock curriculum guides save valuable time, are easy to use, and are highly effective. Each unit begins with a pre-assessment and ends with a post-assessment, so growth and progress can be tracked. Lessons are tied to National and Texas State Standards, freeing teachers to spend more time with students. Each activity is a complete lesson with a focus, closure, extension(s), and suggested assessment opportunities. Differentiated strategies are also identified in every lesson. The evaluation tools are authentic, requiring students to demonstrate knowledge by practical application. Rubrics are provided to help with assessment.

We recognize that one activity cannot reach every student at every ability level, so suggestions are given for modifications. Please feel free to modify activities as needed.

Prufrock curricula are based on conceptual themes. By using abstract words such as *wonders, changes, structures*, and *powers*, the topics are broad, universal, and timeless. Research proves that conceptual learning helps bridge the disciplines requiring higher-order thinking, which in turn leads to meaningful understanding.

Come explore the world of Questions...

"To be, or not to be. That is the question." This may be one of the most famous Shakespearean quotes. In this program, students discover the play from which the quote derived and the context in which it was written. Students learn about Socrates and his ideas about questioning. The "Five Ws" are examined as students gather information to put together a school newspaper. Students examine a new type of comedy as they are challenged to create humorous scenes by only asking questions. Students gain an understanding about how our society has evolved because people in the past were bold enough to ask questions such as, "Do you suppose we can put a man on the moon?"

Acknowledgements

We would like to credit Sandra N. Kaplan, Javits Projects, University of Southern California, for the use of the Depth and Complexity Dimensions in our materials.

A special thank you to Suzy Hagar, Executive Director for Advanced Academic Services in the Carrollton-Farmers Branch Independent School District, for project development advice, suggestions, and support.

Written by: Debbie Keiser, Brenda McGee, Chuck Nusinov, and Mary Hennenfent
Cover Art by: Brandon Bolt
Illustrations: Angie Harrelson
Edited by: Debbie Keiser, Brenda McGee, and Linda Triska

NOTE

The Web sites in this curriculum were working and age-appropriate at the time of publication, but Prufrock Press has no control over any subsequent changes.

Table of Contents

Checklists	Page

Notes

_____

_____

_____

_____

_____

_____

_____

_____

_____

_____

_____

_____

_____

_____

_____

_____

_____

_____

_____

_____

Unit Planner

Concept: Questions
Grade level: 4-6
Length of Time: 40+ hours

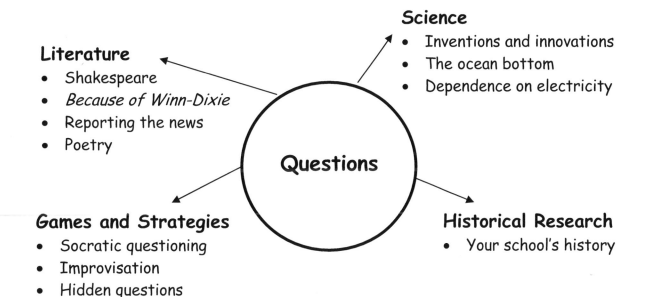

Literature
- Shakespeare
- *Because of Winn-Dixie*
- Reporting the news
- Poetry

Science
- Inventions and innovations
- The ocean bottom
- Dependence on electricity

Questions

Games and Strategies
- Socratic questioning
- Improvisation
- Hidden questions
- 20 questions
- What's my number?
- Past, present and future

Historical Research
- Your school's history

Unit Overview

In the *Questions* curriculum, students will investigate the nature of asking questions and seeking the answers to these questions. Students will explore the curiosity of Shakespeare and Socrates. They will ask questions in order to create a student newspaper, an invention museum and a Jeopardy! style game. Students gain an understanding about how society has evolved because people in the past were bold enough to ask questions.

Enduring Understandings and Generalizations

People are curious.

Curiosity may cause people to ask questions and seek the answers to those questions.

Questioning may drive the evolution of society.

The more people learn, the more curious they may become.

Viewpoints are rarely stagnant.

Guiding Questions for *Questions*

Guiding questions are the factual (F), conceptual (C), and philosophical (P) questions addressed in the curriculum. These are the questions students should be able to answer after completing the activities in this curriculum.

(F) What was the Renaissance period?
(F) What does it take to be a good friend?
(F) What is Socratic questioning?
(F) What are the sections of the newspaper?
(F) What is improvisation?
(F) What is question poetry?
(F) What are hidden questions?
(F) What is a strategy?
(F) Which inventions were discovered by accident?
(F) What is bioluminescence?
(F) What is a viewpoint?

> F= factual question
> C= conceptual question
> P= philosophical question

(C) How did Shakespeare help people understand humanity?
(C) How do you make friends in a new town?
(C) How do facts and opinions differ?
(C) How can a school newspaper sate curiosity about what is happening in your school?
(C) Why is the humor in some improvisation sketches questionable?
(C) How would the world change if nobody was curious?
(C) How could a game strategy apply to real life?
(C) Why is it important to study the bottom of the ocean?
(C) Why have Americans become so dependent on electricity?
(C) How can you build a flashlight?
(C) How can you find information about your school and local history?
(C) How would the world change if everyone had the same viewpoint?

(P) Should students form a plan of action to solve a problem that is considered an adult issue?
(P) Can the past help you predict the future?

Notes

_____

_____

_____

_____

_____

_____

_____

_____

_____

_____

_____

_____

_____

_____

_____

_____

_____

_____

_____

_____

_____

_____

_____

Activity 1 – Pre-Assessment

Differentiation Strategies
Analysis and Synthesis
- Critical Thinking

Multiple Perspectives
- Brainstorming
- Point of View

Instructional Materials
- 5 large sheets of chart paper

Preparation
Write one of the following questions at the top of each piece of chart paper:
- What is a question?
- Why do we ask questions?
- What are some famous questions?
- If you could ask any question and get a definite answer, what would it be and why?
- What are some different kinds of questions?

Place the pieces of chart paper in different areas of the room.

A. Have students form five groups. Assign each group to a piece of chart paper.

B. Inform students they will have 5 minutes at each piece of chart paper to answer the question. Explain that there are no wrong answers. Groups may choose one person to do all the writing, or each student may do his or her own writing. Encourage students to write as many ideas as they can for each question.

C. Give students a signal to begin. After 5 minutes, ask groups to rotate to the next question.

D. After teams have rotated to each of the questions, read each chart and discuss the responses.

E. Save the chart paper for comparison after the Post-Assessment.

Activity 2 – What Did He Mean by That?

Differentiation Strategies
Knowledge and Skills
- Etymology

Analysis and Synthesis
- Creative Problem Solving
- Evaluation

Ethics/Unanswered Questions
- Tolerance for Ambiguity
- Aesthetic Thinking

Communication
- Writing Skills

Instructional Materials
- copies of Attachment 1
- computer with Internet access

Enduring Understanding
The more people learn, the more curious they may become.

Guiding Questions
(F) What was the Renaissance period?
(C) How did Shakespeare help people understand humanity?

Background Information
Perhaps more people would appreciate the writing of William Shakespeare if they understood the time period in which he wrote. He lived during the **Renaissance** period, which was characterized by many developments in art, literature, and technology. The Protestant Church was founded during this period. Many important discoveries led to the knowledge and technology of today. Education became more **prevalent** and people scrambled to learn all they could.

However, some **peasants** continued to cling to the past. They fought change and wanted the world to return to the old ways. They were quickly outnumbered.

Shakespeare lived from 1564 to 1616. His plays are performed and studied today, and he is still considered the world's most popular **playwright**. Shakespeare understood humanity and all aspects of it, both good and evil. He was able to bring to life characters from diverse backgrounds and weave them into believable stories.

As we study Shakespeare today, we are taken with his choice and use of words. Reading Shakespeare is a challenge because we do not speak in this fashion. Perhaps introducing Shakespeare to children in the elementary years will allow them to be more open to his great works when they study him again in high school.

Note

The following Web sites were working and age-appropriate at the time of publication, but Prufrock Press has no control over any subsequent changes. Please preview all sites before letting students view them.

Preparation

Go to the following Web site and locate Sonnet 29. Print the sonnet and make copies for students to read.

http://education.yahoo.com/reference/Shakespeare/poetry/50029.html

A. The following Web site contains the complete script of Shakespeare's "Hamlet."
http://www-tech.mit.edu/Shakespeare/hamlet/hamlet.3.1.html
Scroll down to the speech by Hamlet that begins, "To be or not to be – that is the question." Ask the following questions:

- Judging from the words used by Shakespeare, was this a joyous or dark occasion?
- What does Hamlet mean when he says, "To be or not to be – that is the question"?

B. Tell students that the quote above is one of the most famous lines in a Shakespearean play. Have students brainstorm plays and other quotes they have heard from Shakespeare. Remind students that "Romeo and Juliet" is a play written by Shakespeare. Record responses on the chalkboard.

C. Explain that Shakespeare wrote the play "Hamlet" hundreds of years ago. Share the first three paragraphs of the Background Information, then discuss how Shakespeare's works still convey meaning, even though his writing style is far different from the language we speak today.

D. Distribute copies of Attachment 1. Ask students to form teams of three to examine the quotes from Shakespeare's plays. Encourage students to read each quote and discuss its meaning in today's language. Have students record their ideas on the page. Tell students this activity will be evaluated using the rubric on Attachment 2. Share the attachment with students before they begin.

> ### Teacher Tip
> Rubrics are an effective assessment tool in evaluating student performance in areas which are complex and vague. By allowing students to see what the expectations are before they begin the assignment, work quality improves dramatically.

E. Have students share the results of their discussions. Ask students to discuss whether they enjoy Shakespeare's writing style. Pose the following question: How might Shakespeare have expressed the following sentence, "I was more mad than I had ever been in my life!"?
(Possible answer: "The deep red boiling inside, I knew not this emotion.")

F. Explain that Shakespeare wrote many plays. He wrote comedies and tragedies. Tell students that Shakespeare also wrote 154 sonnets, which are rhyming poems that follow a certain pattern. Write the following rules on the chalkboard:

Each sonnet:
- consists of 14 lines
- is written in **iambic pentameter** (each line has five pairs of syllables)
- has a rhyming pattern that is abab cdcd efef gg

G. Distribute copies of Sonnet 29. Ask students the following questions:
- How many lines are in this sonnet? (14)
- What are the rhyming words? Do they follow the pattern mentioned earlier? (eyes and cries; state and fate; hope and scope; possessed and least; despising and arising; state and gate; brings and kings; yes, they follow the rhyming pattern)
- Why did Shakespeare change the spelling of happily in line 10? (He wanted the line to have 10 syllables.)
- What is poetic license? (Poetic license is permission granted an author or poet to change a word or rule to make it fit his or her purposes.)
- What are the overarching themes of this sonnet? (disgrace, envy, hope, love)

Closure

Challenge students to write sonnets. Remind them to follow the rules for writing sonnets. Encourage students to select a subject and one or several themes before they begin writing. This activity may be assessed using the rubric on Attachment 3. Share this rubric before students begin the assignment.

Extensions

A. Invite students to study other Shakespearean sonnets to discover rhyming patterns, poetic license, and the overarching themes in his writing.

B. Set up a poetry café in your classroom and invite students' family and friends to listen as students read their sonnets. Serve drinks and cookies.

C. Help students select one of Shakespeare's comedies to read as a class. You may want to purchase the Cliff's Notes to help give students background on which to build comprehension.

Assessment

Evaluate each team's ability to work together using the rubric on Attachment 2. Evaluate student-written sonnets and presentations using the rubric on Attachment 3.

Activity 3 – It's All About a Dog

Differentiation Strategies

Knowledge and Skills
- Attributes
- Visualization

Multiple Perspectives
- Brainstorming
- Point of View

Methodology and Use of Resources
- Research

Communication
- Writing Skills

> ## Enduring Understanding
> People are curious.
>
> ## Guiding Questions
> (F) What does it take to be a good friend?
> (C) How do you make friends in a new town?

Instructional Materials
- multiple matching copies of *Because of Winn-Dixie* book, by Kate DiCamillo (at least 1 copy per two students)
- chart paper

Background Information

Because of Winn-Dixie was chosen as a Newbery Honor Book in 2001. This first novel by Kate DiCamillo was inspired by DiCamillo's love of the South. DiCamillo was born in Pennsylvania but moved to Florida when she was 5. She suffered from chronic pneumonia, and doctors thought the mild climate would be good for her. She moved to a small town, much different from Philadelphia. The Southern accent and pace of life caused DiCamillo to fall in love with Florida and eventually led her to write about it.

The protagonist of *Because of Winn-Dixie* is 10-year-old India Opal Buloni. Her father is a preacher when they move to a new town. Opal has no friends. A chance meeting at the grocery store introduces a loveable **mutt** that Opal names Winn-Dixie. With Winn-Dixie on the scene, things begin to happen for Opal, her father, and many other characters in this small town. The book is **lighthearted** and answers many questions such as: How do you make friends in a new town? What does it take to be a good friend? What does 'never judge a book by its cover' really mean?

The book contains some questionable language. Discuss the use of questionable language in the book before reading. Explain to your students that the author assumed a certain maturity level of readers. Preview each chapter before reading and determine whether you will read it as written.

You may choose to read one chapter in combination with another activity from *Questions* during each class meeting.

A. Introduce the book and discuss the Newbery Honor award it received. Ask students to study the cover and read the synopsis on the back. Then have them make predictions about the contents of the book.

B. Invite students to list questions about the book. Write the questions on a piece of chart paper. As students read each chapter, have them return to the list to see if any questions were answered. Encourage students to create more questions as they read.

C. Here are some suggested activities after reading chapters 1 – 4:
Chapter 1 – Have students write a story that answers the question - Where did Winn-Dixie come from? You may want to assess this assignment using the rubric on Attachment 3 or you may have students help you create a rubric using the blank rubric on Attachment 4.

Chapter 2 – Have students discuss the following questions:
What is a Less Fortunate?
Why do you think Opal's father is like a turtle hiding in its shell?
Why do you think the preacher allows Opal to keep the dog?

Chapter 3 – Ask students to write down 10 things they would tell others about their own mother, grandmother, or special caregiver. These things should be special and tell a lot about the person.

Chapter 4 – Have students research the constellations in the night sky. Encourage them to make models of at least 10 constellations and share them with the class.

D. Here are some suggested activities after reading chapters 5 – 8:
Chapter 5 – Ask students to write one question that chapter 5 answers, such as How did Winn-Dixie get to go to church?

Chapter 6 – Have students write predictions about the story Miss Franny Block will tell in Chapter 7.

Chapter 7 – Have students create a title for chapter 7 after reading.

Chapter 8 – Have students create a ledger that Opal might have created showing her installation plan for paying for the leash and collar. Tell students to include the price of each item, the total price, and the amount of money she earned per hour working to pay off her debt.

E. Here are some suggested activities after reading chapters 9 – 12:

Chapter 9 – Have students create character maps of Opal, the preacher, Miss Fanny Block, and Winn-Dixie. Each map should include the character's name and at least four traits of that character.

Chapter 10 – Invite students to create illustrations for chapter 10.

Chapter 11 – Have students research weather patterns in Florida. Encourage them to determine the times during the year when Florida has bad thunderstorms. Discuss the climate of Florida, the amount of rainfall per year, etc.

Chapter 12 – Have students discuss the following questions after reading:
- What does Opal discover about Otis that morning in the pet shop?
- How do Opal and Otis get all the animals back into their cages?
- What new friend does Opal meet when she leaves the pet shop?

F. Here are some suggested activities after reading chapters 13 – 19:
Chapters 13 and 14 – Have students write a composition about the meaning of the following phrase: Don't judge a book by its cover. You may want to assess this assignment using the rubric on Attachment 3 or you may have students help you create a rubric using the blank rubric on Attachment 4.

Chapter 15 - Teach students about allusions. Allusions are references to real events in a fiction story. Ask students to identify an allusion in chapter 15 (the Civil War). Then have them research the causes of the Civil War and present their findings.

Chapters 16 and 17 – Challenge students to retell the life of Littmus W. Block by doing a write-around. To create a write-around, give one student a piece of paper and have him or her write a sentence that begins to tell about the life of Littmus W. Block. Then the student must pass the paper to someone else. That person must write the next sentence. Students continue passing the paper until the story is told. They must do this without talking. When the write-around is complete, ask someone to read it aloud to the class.

Chapters 18 and 19 – Have students discuss the characters' reactions to the Littmus Lozenge.

G. Here are some suggested activities after reading chapter 20 – 25:
Chapter 20 – Ask students what they would plan for a barbecue. Challenge them to develop a menu and entertainment for a party for 10 people. Provide grocery store ads and have students make a list with prices of items needed. Have them determine the approximate amount of money they would spend on the party. When planning is complete, invite students to present their menus and the cost of food.

Chapter 21 – Locate recipes for egg salad and punch, gather the ingredients, and have students follow the recipes to make a snack.

Chapter 22 – Ask students to write about what the preacher means in his prayer when he says, "We appreciate the complicated and wonderful gifts You give us in each other."
Chapter 23 – Before reading chapter 23, have students make predictions about the major event in the chapter. Then have students discuss Gloria Dump's advice: "There ain't no way you can hold on to something that wants to go, you understand? You can only love what you got while you got it."

Chapter 24 – Tell students that Chapter 24 does a great job of describing the layout of Naomi. Challenge students to draw maps of Naomi that include all the major places from the book.

Chapters 25 and 26 – Have students create a list of questions they have about what happens after the story. For example, do Opal and Dunlap become friends? Encourage each student to choose one question to answer by writing another chapter to add to the book. Have students illustrate their chapters and present them to the class when they are finished.

H. Have students complete the Six Hat Thinking activity on Attachment 6.

> **Teacher Tip**
> Six Thinking Hats-created by
> Dr. De Bono in the 1980s.
> White Hat – Facts
> Red Hat – Feeling and emotions
> Black Hat – Judgment and caution
> Yellow Hat – Logical Positive
> Green Hat – Creativity
> Blue Hat – Process Control

Closure
After reading the book, hold a Winn-Dixie discussion group. Ask the following questions to get the discussion started:
• What were the strong points in DiCamillo's writing that made the book believable?
• What could DiCamillo have done to improve the book?
• If there were a sequel, what would it be about?

Extensions
A. Have students write letters to DiCamillo telling her how much they enjoyed her book.

B. Have students read other books by DiCamillo and compare the stories.

Assessment
To assess writing assignments, use the rubric on Attachment 3 or the rubric created by the students. To assess group work, use the rubric on Attachment 2.

Activity 4 - Socratic Questions

Differentiation Strategies

Knowledge and Skills
- Attributes
- Categorizing

Analysis and Synthesis
- Convergent and Divergent Thinking
- Creative Problem Solving

Ethics/Unanswered Questions
- Provocative Questions

Instructional Materials
- computer with Internet access

> ### Enduring Understanding
> Questioning may drive the evolution of society.
>
> ### Guiding Questions
> (F) What is Socratic questioning?
> (C) How do facts and opinions differ?

Background Information

Socrates was an ancient Greek **philosopher**, though many have decided he was more of a teacher. His teaching practices were recorded by Plato. Socrates never wrote anything.

Socrates was known for asking questions. He questioned people around the world about their ideas. He caused people to **reconsider** their thoughts and even made people unsure of their beliefs. This made many people angry, and Socrates was eventually put on trial and **executed** for his practices.

Today, we use Socratic questioning in the classroom to help students re-examine their **hypotheses**. **Socratic questioning** and the **scientific method** have been linked because both follow a similar format: a question, hypothesis, testing, acceptance, retesting, and forming an opinion.

A. Write the following questions on the chalkboard. Have students read and record their answers. (They can use existing journals or spiral notebooks or create one using Attachment 7.)
- What do you want to be when you grow up?
- Should there be universal rules for human rights? Should all humans follow the same rules regarding treatment of other humans? Explain.
- Would you search for the truth about an incident, even if you knew you would not like what you would discover? Why or why not?
- Is cheating in life, school, or business ever the right thing to do? Explain your answer.

B. Group students into four teams. Assign each team one of the questions on the chalkboard. Encourage groups to discuss their questions for several minutes. Have one team member take notes on the discussion.

C. Have students create a list of facts and opinions about their question and the related issues. Have them write what they know and do not know about the issues related to their question.

D. Invite students to research the issues related to their questions using the library or Internet. Explain that when they present their findings they should have some kind of **data**, or information, to back them up. Have students begin to draw conclusions about the best answer to the original question.

E. Have students put all of their information into a presentation format. Encourage them to be creative by making charts or graphs, illustrations, or some kind of visual aid. Require teams to put their ideas into written form to be read and discussed during their presentations. This assignment can be assessed using the Presentation Rubric on Attachment 5 or creating a rubric using Attachment 4.

Closure

Invite teams to present their findings to the class. Begin a class discussion about each question after each presentation.

Extension

Invite teams to trade questions and begin the process again. Compare the answers to the questions after teams have presented for a second time.

Assessment

Use the rubrics selected or created by the students to assess writing and presentations.

Notes

_____

_____

_____

_____

_____

_____

_____

Activity 5 - Six Questions Every Reporter Asks

Differentiation Strategies
Analysis and Synthesis
- Evaluation
- Draw Conclusions

Multiple Perspectives
- Inquiry
- Point of View

Communication
- Writing Skills

Relevance and Significance
- Resource Person

Instructional Materials
- old newspapers (enough for one copy per two students)
- highlighters

Enduring Understanding

People are curious.

Guiding Questions

(F) What are the sections of the newspaper?
(C) How can a school newspaper sate curiosity about what is happening in your school?

A. Review the five W's and the H with students (who, what, where, when, why, how). Explain that every story in the newspaper or on the television news answers these six questions.

B. Distribute newspapers. Have students work in pairs to read three to five **articles** from different **sections** of the newspaper, underlining the five W's and the H within the story. Then have students write a summary of each article on a separate sheet of paper.

Teacher Tip

Invite a guest speaker from your local newspaper. Take students on a field trip to a newspaper office and see the process of producing a newspaper.

C. Ask students to present their summaries for each article.

D. Help students brainstorm activities and events of interest in your school. Then go back to the newspapers and have students identify the different sections of the newspaper. Write the sections of the newspaper on the chalkboard. Then have students sort the activities and events listed earlier into sections of the newspaper.

E. Tell students they will produce a class newspaper with every student producing at least one article. Assess student news articles using the rubric on Attachment 3 or a rubric created by the students.

F. Help students decide what kinds of stories they will include. Encourage them to look for stories that will surprise and entertain readers, such as finding a teacher who spent a summer in Russia or a student who has traveled to all 50 states.

G. Review the interview process. Remind students to create a list of questions before the interview. Be sure students thank the person for his or her time after each interview.

H. Encourage students to edit one another's stories when completed. Then have students print out their stories.

I. Have each student create a puzzle, riddle, or comic strip for the newspaper's fun page.

Closure
Print the stories and fun page and invite students to read the newspaper they produced.

> **Teacher Tip**
> **Bloom's Taxonomy** of learning objectives is the easiest and one of the best ways to **differentiate**. Use your favorite search engine to find and print a chart to keep close. Move your students up the taxonomy by changing your verbs at the **Knowledge, Comprehension, Application, Analysis, Synthesis,** and **Evaluation** levels.

Extensions
A. Have students make copies of the newspaper and distribute them to the teachers in your school. The teachers can place the newspapers in reading centers in their classrooms.

B. Operate a school newspaper as a class. Ask students in other classes to submit stories. Have students create a list of requirements for the stories, puzzles, and other items in the paper. Publish the school newspaper once a month.

Assessment
Assess student news articles using the rubric selected by the students.

Activity 6 - Questionable Humor

Differentiation Strategies
Analysis and Synthesis
- Creative Problem Solving
- Critical Thinking

Multiple Perspectives
- Brainstorming

Relevance and Significance
- Role Playing

Instructional Materials
- copies of Attachment 8

Background Information

Comedy has been popular in the performing arts for hundreds of years. From Shakespeare's comedies to Drew Carey, people of all ages enjoy laughing.

There are schools of acting and comedy all over the United States. Many people try to become professional comedians, but only a select few make it to television. One of the most difficult forms of comedy is **improvisation**. Improvisation means there is no script or memorized act. Improv is **spontaneous**.

By using questions during their routines, some comedians have taken improvisation to a whole new level. They ask for topic ideas from the audience then use the ideas to create spontaneous comedy routines. This takes years of practice and lots of talent.

A. Share the Background Information, then distribute Attachment 8. Invite two students to read the routine aloud.

B. Have students work in pairs to extend the question comedy skits on the attachment. Then invite them to share their responses.

C. Encourage each pair to write a question comedy skit. Have them brainstorm topic ideas and then create their skits.

Enduring Understanding

People are curious.

Guiding Questions

(F) What is improvisation?
(C) Why is the humor in some improvisation sketches questionable?

Closure

Have students present their question skits to the class. Tell students that the Group Evaluation Rubric on Attachment 2 will be used to assess this activity.

Extension

Challenge students to create spontaneous skits in front of the class. Invite two students to the front of the room. Have other students brainstorm topics for the skit. The students doing the skit should select the topic with which they are most comfortable. Remind students that this form of comedy takes lots of practice, but can be done with patience. Have several pairs of students try question comedy.

Assessment

Use the rubric on Attachment 2 to assess group work.

Notes

_____
_____
_____
_____
_____
_____
_____
_____
_____
_____
_____
_____
_____
_____
_____
_____
_____

Activity 7 - Questions in Poetry

Differentiation Strategies
Knowledge and Skills
- Attributes
- Visualization

Analysis and Synthesis
- Aesthetic Thinking
- Creative Problem Solving

Multiple Perspectives
- Brainstorming

Communication
- Writing Skills

Instructional Materials
- assortment of poetry books
- science books
- computer with Internet access

Enduring Understanding
Curiosity may cause people to ask questions and seek the answers to those questions.

Guiding Question
(F) What is question poetry?

A. Remind students that poetry comes in many forms, and that some poems **rhyme** and some do not. There is no set way to write a poem.

B. Invite students to look through the poetry books. Have each student select a poem to share with the class.

C. Tell students they will **compose** their own poetry. Write the following guidelines on the chalkboard to help students write:
- Your poems will be about something in science.
- Each line of your poem will ask a question about your subject.
- Your poem must be at least 10 lines long.
- Your poem does not have to rhyme.

D. Read the below example aloud.

> Do stars shine in the daytime?
> Where is the Big Dipper when it's lunchtime?
> How did the constellations get their names?
> Who discovered the difference between stars and planets?
> Do aliens exist?
> Will we ever live on the moon?
> How many stars have been discovered?
> Are there any other solar systems like ours?
> When did we get the idea to build a space shuttle?
> What did it feel like to walk on the moon?

E. Have students title and illustrate their question poems. Tell students you will use the rubric on Attachment 3 to assess this assignment.

Closure
Invite students to share their question poetry with the class.

Extensions
A. Challenge students to select one or two questions from their poems to research and answer. Provide time on the Internet or in the library for research.

B. Have students write a composition about the questions they asked and the answers they uncovered. Invite students to share their compositions with the class.

C. Have students write more question poetry selecting a different style of poetry. They may use Attachment 9 for ideas.

Assessment
Use the rubric on Attachment 3 to assess student writing.

Notes

_____

_____

_____

_____

_____

_____

Activity 8 - What are Hidden Questions?

Differentiation Strategies
Knowledge and Skills
- Attributes
- Categorizing

Analysis and Synthesis
- Critical Thinking
- Convergent and Divergent Thinking

Multiple Perspectives
- Brainstorming

Methodology and Use of Resources
- Research
- Shares Inquiry

Enduring Understanding
Curiosity may cause people to ask questions and seek the answers to those questions.

Guiding Question
(F) What are hidden questions?

A. Tell students they will brainstorm hidden questions. You will provide an answer and they must provide as many questions as they can. For example: The answer is eggs. What is the question? You would then give students 5 minutes to brainstorm as many questions as they can.

Possible questions:
- Do snakes have eggs or live babies?
- What food besides ham did Sam I Am not like?
- What common food is served with bacon at breakfast?
- What do some children hunt for at Easter?
- What do chickens lay?

B. Write the following statements on the chalkboard one at a time. Have students form teams of three, and allow 5 minutes for each answer.
- The answer is 30. What is the question?
- The answer is Australia. What is the question?
- The answer is Dr. Seuss. What is the question?
- The answer is smile. What is the question?
- The answer is 100. What is the question?
- The answer is 60. What is the question?

C. You may use these as introductory activities each time the class meets.

Closure

Ask students to **evaluate** the most creative questions. Then have them discuss the most difficult part of the exercise.

Extension

Give students 5 minutes to generate their own list of answers. Use their lists of ideas before class begins or when class ends each day.

Assessment

Evaluate group work using Attachment 2.

Notes

Activity 9 – 20 Questions

Differentiation Strategies
Knowledge and Skills
- Attributes
- Categorizing

Demonstration
- Analysis and Synthesis
- Creative Problem Solving

Ethics/Unanswered Questions
- Provocative Questions

Enduring Understanding
People are curious.

Guiding Question
(C) How would the world change if nobody was curious?

Background Information
The game 20 Questions is typically played with one person thinking about or spying something and the other players asking yes-or-no questions to find the answer.

In this activity, students will **modify** the game to make it more challenging.

A. Play a game of 20 Questions with students. Select an item in your classroom for students to guess. Remind students they may only ask yes-or-no questions. All other questions should be answered with, "I don't know." Remind students to think of **strategies** and to listen carefully to the questions being asked.

B. When the game is over, ask students the following questions:
- What is the most important factor in playing 20 questions?
- What is the easiest mistake to make?
- What are some of the strategies you use when you play the game?
- How could the game be changed?

C. Instruct students to create their own versions of the game. Encourage them to use the ideas discussed in the last question.

D. Have students form teams of three. Allow 30 to 45 minutes for them to plan and run simulations of their enhanced games. When their games are perfected, ask them to write down the rules and steps to playing their game.

E. Invite teams to present their new games to the class. Have each team present the change and rules it created, then play the modified game.

Closure

Have students write about the following question: Do you think it is more difficult to modify an existing game or to create a new game? Explain your answer. Have students create a rubric to assess this assignment.

Extensions

A. Have students select a popular board game to modify. Encourage them to keep the same pieces to the game, but to change the board and rules.

B. Invite students to share their modified games with the class.

C. Invite students to visit the following Web site to play a computer version of 20 Questions. Have students play the game several times to try to determine how the game works. As always, please preview all sites before allowing student access. **http://www.20q.net/**

D. Have students try to answer the following questions as they play the game:
- At what point do you think the computer knows the object?
- Does the computer ask silly questions to throw you off? Why?
- Are there certain questions the computer asks every time? What are they?

Assessment

Use the rubric created by the students to assess the Closure activity.

Notes

Activity 10 - What's My Number?

Differentiation Strategies

Knowledge and Skills
- Attributes
- Demonstration

Analysis and Synthesis
- Creative Problem Solving
- Critical Thinking

Communication
- Decision Making

Instructional Materials
- dry erase board and marker

Enduring Understanding
The more people learn, the more curious they may become.

Guiding Questions
(F) What is a strategy?
(C) How could a game strategy apply to real life?

Background Information
Game strategy is the science of planning and maneuvering into the most advantageous position so you will beat your opponent. It is a plan of action carefully laid out before you actually make a move.

The rules for the game What's My Number? are similar to 20 Questions. One person thinks of a number in a **specified** range, for example between 0 and 5,000. Then other players ask yes-or-no questions to help find the number.

Sample questions: Is it an odd number? Is it between 1,000 and 2,000? Is it a two-digit number?

A. Share the Background Information, then play What's My Number? Keep track of **relevant** information on the dry erase board. For example, information you might write for the three questions above might be:
- not odd
- between 1,000 and 2,000
- not a two-digit number

B. When students guess the number, **tally** the number of questions asked. Keep track of the number of questions asked with each game played.

C. Ask students the following questions after several games:

- What strategies did you use to play the game?
- What were some good questions to ask?
- Which questions were not so good?
- Do you think the class improved in the number of questions asked with each game? Explain your answer.

D. Have students construct line graphs showing each game and the numbers of questions asked. See the example below

Questions asked during What's My Number?

Questions Asked:

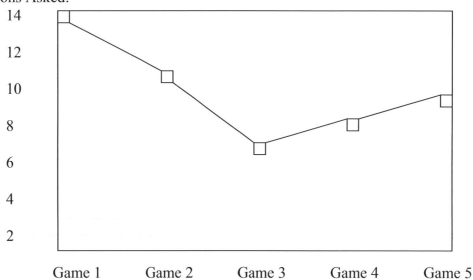

E. Have students determine the **average** number of questions asked per game by adding the number of questions asked in all games and dividing by the number of games played.

F. Play the game one more time and challenge students to beat the average. Ask students to develop a game strategy before they play again.

G. Ask students to discuss whether strategies help when playing this game. Invite students to discuss strategies again. Play the game again, allowing students to discuss each question as a class before asking it.

Closure

Have students write a paragraph explaining how learning game strategies could help you in a real life situation using examples. Have students create a rubric by which this assignment will be assessed.

Extensions

A. Ask students to modify this game to make it more challenging or simpler. Invite students to present modified games to the class.

B. Have students share their modified games with other classes.

C. Challenge students to modify the game to use words instead of numbers. Ask them to tell how the questions would change.

Assessment

Assess the Closure Activity using the rubric created by the students.

Notes

_____

_____

_____

_____

_____

_____

_____

_____

_____

_____

_____

_____

_____

_____

_____

_____

_____

Differentiation Strategies

Knowledge and Skills
- Demonstration
- Classifying

Analysis and Synthesis
- Evaluation
- Generalizations

Multiple Perspectives
- Brainstorming

Communication
- Research

Enduring Understanding
Questioning may drive the evolution of society.

Guiding Question
(F) Which inventions were discovered by accident?

Instructional Materials
- computer with Internet access
- one or several of the following books:

Mistakes That Worked by Charlotte Foltz Jones
Brainstorm!: The Stories of Twenty American Kid Inventors by Tom Tucker
Accidents May Happen: 50 Inventions Discovered by Mistake by Charlotte Fultz Jones
The Kid Who Invented the Popsicle: And Other Surprising Stories About Inventions by Don L. Wulffson

Background Information

Did you know the Popsicle™ was once called an Epsicle, and was invented by a child during a freak freeze in San Francisco? Did you know that Post-It™ notes were invented by accident? That the idea for Velcro™ came from sticker burrs? During this eye-opening activity, students will have the opportunity to discover how many other common items were invented by accident. Speaking of eye-opening, did you know glasses were invented in the 1200s?

A. Tell students they will put together an invention **museum** for other classes to tour. They will use the resources gathered as well as Internet sites listed for their research.

B. Allow time for students to explore the following Web sites to learn more about inventions and their inventors. As always, please preview all sites before letting students view them.
http://www.cbc.ca/kids/general/the-lab/history-of-invention/default.html
http://www.pbs.org/wgbh/amex/telephone/sfeature/

C. Allow students to browse through the books you collected.

D. Have students share their favorite discoveries about inventions and inventors. Make a list of favorites on the chalkboard. When students are finished sharing, assign one invention and inventor to each student.

E. Have students research the assigned invention and inventor in depth. Ask each student to write or type a one-page story about the inventor, how he or she got the idea for the invention, and how he or she carried out plans to develop and sell the invention (if applicable). Each story should be titled in question format. For example, *How Was the Popsicle Invented?* or *Do you Know Who Invented the Ball Point Pen?* Invite students to create a rubric to assess their projects using Attachment 4.

F. If possible, have students gather pictures of the actual items to display with their stories. If there are no pictures and they cannot get the item, have students draw the item.

G. Have students invite other classes to the invention museum. Each student should stand by his or her story and be available to answer questions.

Closure
Have students make generalizations about inventors and inventions. A rubric for this task is on Attachment 11.

Extensions
Encourage students to ask permission for your school to host an invention competition. Have them present the idea to the school board for **approval**, send invitations to other schools, and organize the competition.

Assessment
A. Use the rubric on Attachment 11 to evaluate the Closure Activity.

B. Use the rubric created by students in Step E to assess projects.

Notes

Activity 12 - What's on the Bottom?

Differentiation Strategies
Knowledge and Skills
- Research
- Visualization

Communication
- Demonstration

Relevance and Significance
- Resource Person

Enduring Understanding
Curiosity may cause people to ask questions and seek the answers to those questions.

Guiding Questions
(F) What is bioluminescence?
(C) Why is it important to study the bottom of the ocean?

Instructional Materials
- *Fountains of Life: The Story of Deep-Sea Vents* book, by Elizabeth Tayntor Gowell
- *Slippery, Splendid Sea Creatures* book, by Madelyn Wood Carlisle
- computer with Internet access
- other books, videos, or audiotapes about life at the bottom of the ocean.

Background Information
The deepest part of the ocean is almost 7 miles below the surface. It is located in the Pacific Ocean near Guam in the **Marianas Trench**. Until 1960, no one knew if life existed at the bottom of the ocean. The Navy built a special submarine to withstand enormous **pressure** and sent it to the bottom of the ocean. The trip took almost 5 hours, but at last the men saw the ocean floor. As they looked carefully they began to see sparkles and tiny lights in the deep water. They soon realized they were seeing life at the bottom of the ocean. Many of the fish that live in the **twilight zone** of the ocean give off light. This light is called **bioluminescence**. These fish have organs that glow in the dark. Scientists estimate 90 percent of the creatures living at these depths are bioluminescent.

A. Invite students to brainstorm everything they know about life at the bottom of the ocean. Record their responses on the chalkboard.

B. Read the Background Information aloud. Ask students to discuss other things that are bioluminescent. (fireflies, some forms of seaweed)

C. Encourage students to learn more about the creatures of the deep by reading the books you collected or visiting some or all of the Web sites below. As always, please preview all sites before letting students view them.
http://tqjunior.thinkquest.org/4106/
http://www.seasky.org/monsters/sea7a1.html
http://www.pbs.org/wgbh/nova/abyss/life/bestiary.html

D. Have each student choose an aspect of life on the ocean floor to research. Here are some topic ideas.

- a fish living at the bottom of the ocean
- the geography of the ocean floor
- submersibles that travel to the ocean floor
- a current study taking place at the bottom of the ocean
- the Marianas Trench
- deep-sea vents

E. Have students write a script for a documentary about what they chose to research. Encourage students to create props and other visuals to go with their scripts. Share with students what you are going to assess during this activity. You may want to assess writing and group work using Attachment 2 and Attachment 3 and/or presentations using Attachment 5.

Closure
Invite students to present their documentaries to the class.

Extensions
A. Have students videotape their documentaries, then have them create a simple quiz that can be taken after watching their video. Help students develop the test and an answer key. Make the videotape and quiz available for teachers to check out in the library.

B. Invite students to decorate the classroom to look like the bottom of the ocean. Here are some suggestions:

- cover the lights with blue cellophane
- using research about fish at the bottom of the ocean, have students create three-dimensional fish to hang from the ceiling
- cover tables and chairs with paper or old sheets to simulate the topography of the ocean floor

C. Invite other classes to see the room. Have students become living exhibits telling about the part of the ocean in which they live, describing life there, telling how they get food, etc.

Assessment
Assess writing and group work using Attachment 2 and Attachment 3. Use Attachment 5 to assess the presentations.

Activity 13 – How Is Together Better?

Differentiation Strategies
Knowledge and Skills
- Attributes

Analysis and Synthesis
- Creative Problem Solving

Multiple Perspectives
- Paradoxes
- Group Consensus

Communication
- Decision Making

Enduring Understanding
Viewpoints are rarely stagnant.

Guiding Questions
(F) What is a viewpoint?
(C) How would the world change if everyone had the same viewpoint?
(P) Should students form a plan of action to solve a problem that is considered an adult issue?

Instructional Materials
- 1 package of 3 x 5 index cards
- sticky notes
- copies of Attachment 10

A. Read students the following problem:
A local developer wants to drain a pond, **demolish** an old playground, and cut down many trees near the school. He plans to build a garden supply store. The school uses the pond to gather water samples, mosquito **larvae**, and other creatures. The teachers take students to the park for picnics and reading **excursions**. The trees and pond help the **environment** and the creatures living in the park. Students and teachers at the school do not want the old park torn down. What can they do?

B. Tell students it is their job to develop a solution to this problem, without discussing ideas with one another. Give them 2 or 3 minutes to brainstorm several solutions. Have students write each solution on an index card.

C. Have students form teams of four. Ask students to share their ideas with team members. Encourage students to discuss the problem and their solutions with one another for 20 minutes. Have teams develop and enhance the original solutions and write new solutions on new index cards.

D. Invite each team to present its ideas. Then allow the class time to decide on the five best possible solutions. Each solution should be written on an index card.

E. Place the index cards on different tables around the room. Invite students to read the five solutions.

F. Tell students to evaluate the solutions based on a 100-point scale. The solution they like the best should receive the most points and the solution they like least should receive the fewest points.

G. Give each student five sticky notes. Have students divide their points between the five solutions. When voting has finished, assign two students to each solution to tabulate the points. Announce the winning solution.

H. Have students gather their original solutions and hang them on the wall. Then have them hang up the solutions that were developed by the small teams. Finally have them hang up the five solutions created by the class. Discuss the similarities and differences between the complexities of the groups of solutions. Have students discuss the saying "two heads are better than one."

Closure

Have students write a persuasive paragraph stating their opinion about whether or not children should form a plan of action to try and solve a problem that is considered an adult issue. Have students create a rubric by which this assignment should be assessed. Students should decide on the minimum number of reasons to support their opinion to earn the highest grade.

Extensions

A. Introduce students to debate, a formal way to discuss two-sided issues. Make copies of Attachment 10 and have students study the debate process. Use the winning solution to debate pro and con. Have students form teams of four. The affirmative teams will argue in support of the solution. Negative teams will argue against the solution. When teams are prepared, hold the debate. Students not debating can be judges. Have them create a judge's record sheet as seen on Attachment 10.

B. Have students brainstorm current problems in your classroom, school, or district. Encourage students to choose one problem to discuss.

C. Have students repeat the solution process. Then have students write a proposal to the authority or authorities whom their solution directly affects (i.e. principal, other teachers, school board, etc.). Send the proposal and convey the response to students when you get it.

Assessment

Assess the Closure activity using the rubric created by students.

Activity 14 - Who Turned Out the Lights?

Differentiation Strategies
Analysis and Synthesis
- Creative Problem Solving
- Trend Extrapolation

Ethics/Unanswered Questions
- Provocative Questions
- Tolerance for Ambiguity

Multiple Perspectives
- Brainstorming

Enduring Understanding
Questioning may drive the evolution of society.

Guiding Question
(C) Why have Americans become so dependent on electricity?

Instructional Materials
- computer with Internet access
- books about inventions

Background Information
Some teachers still remember life without calculators, portable phones, microwaves, VCRs, video games, etc. Some teachers remember life without televisions, let alone color TV sets. This activity causes students to think about what life would be like without one of these **comforts**. What would life be like, for example, if electricity had never been **harnessed**? Students will choose one **technological** development and brainstorm the ramifications of not having that item in today's society. They will determine what other aspects of life would be affected.

A. Begin this activity by telling students a story about your life without some form of technology readily available today. Below is an example.

Once upon a time, I lived in a world that had no _____. Can you imagine living without _____ today? Instead of using _____ we had to _____. (List other ways life was different without this development in technology.)

B. Place students in teams of three. Have students brainstorm a list of technological advances they could not live without (television, video games, DVD players, etc.) Allow students to brainstorm for at least 10 minutes.

C. Invite teams to share their brainstorming with the class. Then ask the following question: How many of these things that you could not live without depend on electricity? Have students circle each item on their lists that would be affected. Have students share their lists.

D. Lead a class discussion about the importance of electricity in our lives. Then ask students to list several important things that were invented as a result of electricity (light bulbs, electric can openers, toasters, etc.)

E. Ask the following question: What if light bulbs had never been invented? Have students brainstorm all of the things we would not be able to use today if we had to depend on the light bulb (computer screens, blinkers on the car, lighting our homes, etc.)

F. Have students select one invention or innovation about which to research. Students should find and report the following information:
- Who invented or discovered it?
- When did this happen?
- What other developments resulted as a response to this invention?

G. Have students write a separate composition about how our lives would be affected if this object had never been invented. Encourage students to brainstorm the ramifications from all angles. Have students select a rubric to use for this assignment or create a new one.

Closure
Invite students to share their reports and compositions with the class.

Extensions
A. Have students imagine life 30 years from now. Ask what new inventions and developments will take place in our near future.

B. Encourage students to write about and illustrate a future development in technology that will affect their lives. This development should be something that will cause their children to look back and say, "I don't know how you lived without it!"

Assessment
Have students help you develop a checklist of each item to be completed during this activity. As students complete the item, check it off the list.

Notes

_____

_____

_____

_____

_____

Activity 15 - How Does It Work?

Differentiation Strategies
Knowledge and Skills
- Attributes
- Visualization

Analysis and Synthesis
- Analogies
- Evaluation
- Creative Thinking

Multiple Perspectives
- Brainstorming

Instructional Materials
- several simple items for students to disassemble and reassemble (3 flashlights, spring-loaded ball point pen, mechanical pencil)
- working string of holiday lights
- (6) 9-volt batteries
- 6 pieces of duct tape
- wire strippers
- wire cutters
- copies of Attachments 12 and 13

Background Information
A **discovery** is something that is new. An **invention** is something a person creates. An **innovation** takes place when someone adds to an invention or combines it with something else to create a new object.

Simple machines were invented thousands of years ago. Most things with moving parts inside are based on the six simple machines: wheel and axle, pulley, inclined plane, wedge, gears, and levers. This means most things being developed today are not inventions, but innovations.

The flashlight is an innovation. It is made of a **circuit** containing a light bulb (thank you, Thomas Edison), a **conductor** made of wire (thank you, Benjamin Franklin) and a plastic or metal casing. The flashlight is the results of hard work by many inventors and innovators.

The ideas behind many inventions and innovations usually come out of necessity. The flashlight, for example, probably came from the need for a portable, non-flammable light source. Carrying a lighted candle into a barn full of hay was not the best idea.

By taking apart a flashlight and then building their own flashlight, students will begin to see how innovations are made. They will be challenged to take the components of a flashlight and create something new, an innovation.

Preparation

Use the wire cutters to cut the holiday light string into small pieces, leaving 1 bulb between several inches of wire. Use the wire strippers to strip a 1-inch segment of the plastic insulation off either end of each holiday light segment.

A. Give each team a working flashlight and a copy of Attachment 12. Instruct students to follow the directions on Attachment 12.

B. Share the Background Information. Then ask students the following questions:
- What are the components of a flashlight that make it work? (bulb, battery, casing)
- What happens when you touch the bulb directly to the battery? (nothing, because you do not complete the circuit)

C. Explain that the path electricity flows through is called a circuit. A circuit must be complete for the bulb to light. Ask the following question: What does a light switch do when you flip it to the on position? (It completes the circuit.)

D. Complete the following circuit experiment:
Sit with students in a circle with hands on their knees, palms up.
- Have each student place his or her left hand on top of the right hand of the person to his or her left.
- Start the "flow" of electricity by taking your left hand and gently slapping the hand of the person to your right. Have student continue until the circuit is completed once around the circle.
- Then, scoot out of the circle and have students repeat the experiment without closing the gap. They will not be able to complete the circuit because one person has been removed.
- Have students discuss analogies that can be made between this game and flipping a light switch on and off. Example: complete : incomplete :: light : dark

E. Tell students they can make homemade circuits now. Distribute copies of Attachment 13 and have students gather the supplies. Instruct students to follow the instructions on the attachment to make their own circuits. Tell them they will be assessed using the Group Evaluation Rubric.

F. Have students discuss how they could build their own flashlights using the circuit they created. Then allow time for students to gather supplies and construct flashlights. Challenge students to devise a way to make a switch that can be turned off and on.

Closure

A. Lead students in a discussion comparing their flashlights to the actual flashlights.

B. Challenge students to imagine they are living during the time electric lights are being created and sold for the first time. Have them create a time line telling how they spent their days before the invention of the light bulb and another time line telling how they spent their days after they acquired electric lighting for their home. Have students create a rubric to assess their time lines before beginning.

C. Have students create a Venn diagram comparing houses without electric lights to houses with electric lighting. How would activities inside the home have been alike and different?

Extension

Challenge students to use the components of the flashlights they created to make another innovation. Invite students to present their innovations to the class.

Assessment

A. Make note of interesting ideas shared during the Closure discussion.

B. Use the rubric created in Step B of the Closure to assess student time lines.

Notes

_____

_____

_____

_____

_____

_____

_____

_____

_____

_____

_____

Activity 16 - Answers Before Questions?

Differentiation Strategies
Knowledge and Skills
- Research

Multiple Perspectives
- Shared Inquiry
- Brainstorming

Relevance and Significance
- Resource Person

Enduring Understanding
Curiosity may cause people to ask questions and seek the answers to those questions.

Guiding Question
(C) How can you find information about your school and local history?

Instructional Materials
- 3 bells
- resources about the history of your school and school district – videotapes, audiotapes, people to interview, records from the school district, etc.

Background Information
Jeopardy!© is a game that has been played for many years on television. The **premise** is for players to listen to a clue and **pose** the correct answer in the form of a question. As students create their own elementary school Jeopardy! game, they will learn about the history of their school and district, as well as how to create and play Jeopardy!

A. Ask students the following questions:
- Who was the first principal at our school?
- When was our school built?
- When was our school district founded?
- How old are the first students who graduated from our school now?
- What is the most exciting thing that ever happened in our school? In our school district?

B. Tell students they will learn the answers to most or all of these questions as they research the foundations of your school and district. Ask students to brainstorm places where this kind of information might be available (local library, school library, city hall, school district administration office, historians for the school district, teachers who have been in the district many years, etc.)

C. Assign teams of students to uncover information about the following questions:
- When was the school district founded?
- Who founded it?
- Where was the first school and what was it called?

- How many students were in it?
- Who was the first principal?
- Who were the first teachers?
- Did the school have a school song? What was it?
- Any other interesting information.

D. Invite people from the community to speak and be interviewed about the history of the school and the district.

E. When all information has been gathered, tell students they will create a Jeopardy! game that could be played by other classes or teachers during a school wide assembly.

F. Students should write the answers and questions for the Single Jeopardy! and Double Jeopardy! rounds.

Closure
Have students present their answers and questions to the class. Then ask students to write a brief history of their school. Have students create a rubric by which this assignment can be assessed.

Extension
Encourage students to plan and implement an assembly for the entire school. They can use the answers they created to make a real Jeopardy! game. Here are some helpful hints:
- Find and clear a large wall in a large room for the assembly. (cafeteria or gym)
- Write the answers to be read to players on index cards and on pieces of chart paper. Have students brainstorm other ways this could be done (using an overhead projector, etc.).
- Students should present their ideas for an assembly to the principal. They should write a **persuasive** letter, stressing the educational value of students learning about the origins of the school and district while attending an entertaining assembly.

Assessment
Assess the Closure activity using the rubric created by the students.

Notes

_____

_____

_____

_____

_____

_____

Activity 17 – Questions of the Past, Present, Future

Differentiation Strategies
Analysis and Synthesis
- Draw Conclusions
- Creative Problem Solving
- Trend Extrapolation

Ethics/Unanswered Questions
- Futuristics
- Evaluate Situations

Multiple Perspectives
- Brainstorming

Communication
- Writing Skills

Instructional Materials
- several sheets of chart paper

Enduring Understanding
Questioning may drive the evolution of society.

Guiding Question
(P) Can the past help you predict the future?

Background Information
The world is the way it is today because people are curious. Throughout the ages, people have wondered whether we would ever set foot on the moon, and how fast people can travel. It seems as soon as the questions are posed, someone begins work finding the answer.

In this activity, students will determine some important questions posed by our **ancestors**, and they will ask questions to be answered someday by our **descendants**. Tell students they will be evaluated on their group participation using the rubric on Attachment 2.

A. Read the Background Information aloud, and direct students to the pieces of chart paper. Ask students to imagine they are living hundreds, even thousands of years ago. What kinds of questions might our ancestors have asked about our world, life, etc? Allow time for students to brainstorm and write their questions on chart paper.

B. Have students share the questions they brainstormed. Then ask them to brainstorm questions they have today, such as: *Will we ever go to Mars?* or *Will we ever have technology that will allow us to travel anyplace instantly such as a time machine?* Record answers on the chalkboard.

C. Ask students the following question: What do you think people 100 years from now will be wondering? Have students brainstorm a list of questions people in the next **century** might ask.

Closure

Lead students in a discussion about how they think the age of a person might affect the way a person would answer any one of these three questions.

- Do you think man will ever land on Mars?
- Could you live a normal life without a cell phone?
- Do you think using the Internet might be an invasion of your privacy?

Extensions

A. Have students survey younger and older classes using the same three questions they answered. Then have them compare the answers and discuss the difference age makes in the answers.

B. Have students interview parents and grandparents using the same three questions. Discuss the differences in **perspectives**.

Assessment

Use the rubric on Attachment 2 to evaluate group work.

Notes

Activity 18 - Post-Assessment

Differentiation Strategies
Analysis and Synthesis
- Critical Thinking

Multiple Perspectives
- Brainstorming

Instructional Materials
- 5 large sheets of chart paper

Preparation
Write one of the following questions at the top of each piece of chart paper:
- What are the reasons we ask questions?
- What are some famous questions?
- If you could ask any question and get a definite answer, what would it be and why?
- What are some different kinds of questions?
- What are some questions that will be asked in the future?

Place the pieces of chart paper in different areas of the room.

A. Have students form five groups. Assign each group to a piece of chart paper.

B. Inform students they will have 5 minutes to answer the question at each piece of chart paper. Remind students there are no wrong answers. Groups may choose for one person to do all the writing or each student may do his or her own writing. Encourage students to write as many ideas on each question as they can.

C. Give students a signal to begin. After 5 minutes, ask groups to rotate to the next question.

D. After all teams have rotated to each of the questions, read each chart and discuss the responses. Compare responses to the Pre-Assessment used at the beginning of the unit.

Notes

_____

_____

_____

_____

_____

_____

_____

_____

_____

_____

_____

_____

_____

_____

_____

_____

_____

_____

_____

_____

_____

_____

_____

Directions:

Read the following quotes from Shakespeare's writing. Discuss what Shakespeare was saying in each quote and express his quote in language from today.

Parting is such sweet sorrow.

Conscience does make cowards of us all.

Be great in act, as you have been in thought.

Conceit in weakest bodies works the strongest.

My age is as a lusty winter, frosty but kindly.

For nothing can seem foul to those that win.

I wasted time, and now time doth waste me.

My conscience hath a thousand several tongues, and every tongue brings in a several tale, and every tale condemns me for a villain.

Life every man holds dear; but the dear man holds honor far more precious dear than life.

Ambition should be made of sterner stuff.

Thou art all ice. They kindness freezes.

The devil can cite Scripture for his purpose.

When we are born we cry that we are come to this great stage of fools.

Student or Team: _____

Assignment: _____

Directions: Mark the appropriate rating for each criterion. Use these individual ratings to assign an overall rating for the assignment.

Criteria	0 Working on it!	1 Novice	2 Acceptable	3 Out of the Box!	Not Applicable
Worked Well Together	Could not work as a team to complete a task	Worked together part of the time with much guidance from the teacher to complete the task	Worked with the team with little assistance from the teacher and completed the task	Worked well with the team with no assistance from the teacher and completed the task	N/A
Looks Like	Working separately, not talking about the task, not sharing ideas	Working together little, beginning to share ideas and ask questions	Working together part of the time, asking questions, and sharing ideas	Working together all the time, heads together, concentrating on task, smiles	N/A
Sounds Like	Off task, quiet or arguing, not talking about assignment	Talking some about assignment, with other off-task conversation	Conversation mostly about assignment, sharing questions and ideas	Conversation is about assignment, sharing questions, ideas, and evaluating the project	N/A
OVERALL					

Comments:

Student or Team: _____

Assignment: _____

Directions: Mark the appropriate rating for each criterion. Use these individual ratings to assign an overall rating for the assignment.

Criteria	0 Working on it!	1 Novice	2 Acceptable	3 Out of the Box!	Not Applicable
Uses Pre-writing strategies	Cannot generate pre-writing graphic organizers, notes, or brain-storming	Some use of pre-writing in the form of organizers, notes, or brainstorming	Use of more than one pre-writing strategy; mostly well-organized and thought out	Numerous strategies used and followed to create a well-organized and thought-out composition	N/A
Content is valid and accurate	Content is weak and shows little insight	Content is accurate but lacks insight; few supporting examples	Content is accurate with some questions left unanswered and a few supporting examples	Content is 100 percent accurate and has supporting examples	N/A
Organization	Not organized	Somewhat organized	Very organized	Organization far exceeded the standards	N/A
Oral Presentation of information	Could not express or present information	Presentation lacked creativity and was not very informative	Presentation moderately creative, entertaining, and informative	Engaging presentation that was creative, entertaining, and informative	N/A
OVERALL					

Comments:

Attachment 4   Blank Evaluation Rubric

Student or Group: _____

Assignment: _____

Criteria	0 Working on It!	1 Novice	2 Acceptable	3 Out of the Box!

Comments

Attachment 5				Presentation Rubric	

Student or Team: _____

Assignment: _____

Directions: Mark the appropriate rating for each criterion. Use these individual ratings to assign an overall rating for the assignment.

RATINGS	0 Working on it!	1 Novice	2 Acceptable	3 Out of the Box!	Not Applicable
Content	Did not stay on topic	Stayed on topic for most of presentation	Stayed on topic and demonstrated some elaboration	Stayed on topic with extensive elaboration and application	N/A
Oral Expression	Could not express ideas	Could only express some ideas	Easy to understand	Very well articulated	N/A
Organization	Not organized	Somewhat organized	Very organized	Organization far exceeded the standards	N/A
Preparation	Outline incomplete	Outline or preparation didn't represent entire project	Outline complete, props complete	Outline complete and well-organized, exemplary props	N/A
OVERALL					

Comments:

Directions: Analyze Because of Winn Dixie using DeBono's Six Thinking Hats.

WHITE HAT

List three facts you learned about living in Florida.

1.

2.

3.

BLACK HAT

What emotional problems and feelings did Opal have after her
   mother's death and moving to a new place?

RED HAT

How does Opal feel about Dunlap at the end of the book?

BLUE HAT

What will Opal do after the story ends?

GREEN HAT

What one thing would you have done differently if you had been there in Opal's place?

YELLOW HAT

What do you think people learn from reading this book? What do you think the author was trying to teach us?

Instructional Materials
- 1 large sheet of construction paper per student
- 30 sheets of paper (lined or unlined) per student
- hole punch
- yarn

Instructions

1. Fold a large sheet of construction paper in half, like a book.

2. Create a journal cover, then glue it onto the front page of the construction paper book.

3. Place 30 pages of paper inside the construction paper book. Stack the edges evenly against the fold. Close the notebook.

4. Holding the paper tightly so it doesn't slide, make 3 hole punches along the bind. Loop each hole with a piece of yarn. Knot and tie in a bow.

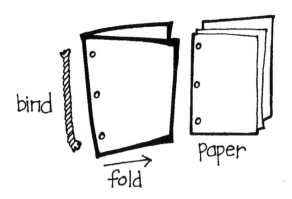

Journal 2

Instructional Materials
- 10 large pieces of construction paper per student (assorted colors)
- 30 pieces of paper (lines or unlined) per student
- hole punch
- stapler
- yarn

Instructions
1. Place a piece of construction paper on the table. Fold a pocket and staple the sides.

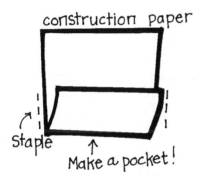

2. Add pieces of white paper

3. Punch holes and bind with yarn or string.

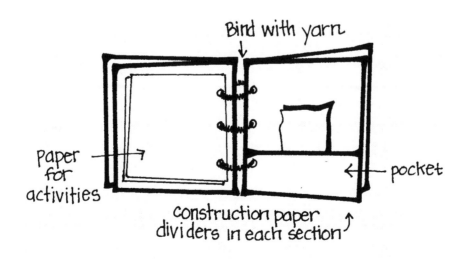

Directions

Read the comedy skits below. This skit may not seem very funny because it is already written for you. The humor behind question comedy is watching the comedians devise ways to have a conversation by only asking questions.

Try to extend each skit by devising questions that would fit into the conversation.

Topic: **Ordering a hamburger at a restaurant**

Person 1:   What kind of hamburgers do you have?
Person 2:   Would you like to see a menu?
Person 1:   Can we get some drinks first?
Person 2:   How about some tea?
Person 1:   Can we get lemon with that?
Person 2:   Would you like fresh or lemon juice concentrate?
Person 1:   Are fresh lemons in season now?
Person 2:
Person 1:
Person 2:
Person 1:

Topic: **Looking for something in a grocery store**

Person 1:   Can you help me find something?
Person 2:   What are you looking for?
Person 1:   What are those things called that you use to brush your teeth?
Person 2:   Are you talking about toothbrushes?
Person 1:   Aren't they located near the toothpaste?
Person 2:
Person 1:
Person 2:
Person 1:
Person 2:

Topic: **Small child doesn't want to go to bed**

Person 1:   Have you brushed your teeth yet?
Person 2:   Aaw, is it time for bed?
Person 1:   What did I tell you?
Person 2:   Do I have to take a bath?
Person 1:   Are you telling me you haven't had a bath yet?
Person 2:   Didn't I tell you that I was watching my favorite show tonight?
Person 1:
Person 2:
Person 1:
Person 2:

Now create an original skit of your own. Select a topic and be sure each person in your skit asks only questions.

   Brainstormed Topic Ideas:

Haiku:
An unrhymed verse of 3 lines, 5, 7, and 5 syllables respectively, all with the same thought.

Cinquain:
A 5-line poem.
Line 1 = 1 word title;
Line 2 = 2 words describing title;
Line 3 = 3 words of feelings describing title;
Line 4 = 4 words of showing action for title; and
Line 5 = 5 different words that are synonyms for the title.

Chain Verse:
The last word or phrase of each line becomes the beginning of the next.

Diamante:
Poetry in the shape of a diamond with 7 lines.
Pattern One:
Line 1 = one subject noun;
Line 2 = 2 adjectives related to line 1;
Line 3 = 3 participles ("ing" words) related to line 1;
Line 4 = 4 word phrases that make a transition from the idea of line 1 to the idea of line 7;
Line 5 = 3 participles ("ing" words) related to line 7;
Line 6 = 2 adjectives related to line 7; and
Line 7 = one noun, opposite in meaning to the subject of line 1.

Pattern Two:
Lines 1 and 7 = Synonyms (nouns)
Line 4 = 4 word phrase describing the subject

Concrete (Geometric):
Poetry that looks like the object written about.

Tanka:
A similar form of poetry to Haiku. The syllables are the most important thing. It can be used to accompany a slide show, geography lesson, or environmental concept.
Line 1 = 5 syllables;
Line 2 = 7 syllables;
Line 3 = 5 syllables;
Line 4 = 7 syllables; and
Line 5 – 7 syllables.

Blank Verse (Free Verse):
A form of poetry that does not rhyme.

Triante (Triangle Poetry):
Poetry that takes the shape of a triangle because of the length of its lines.
Title = 1 word (other words refer to the title)
Line 1 = 2 words (smells)
Line 2 = 3 words (touch)
Line 3 = 4 words (sights)
Line 4 = 5 words (sounds)

Concentric Circles:
The words of the poem follow a spiral or series of concentric circles.

Room Setup

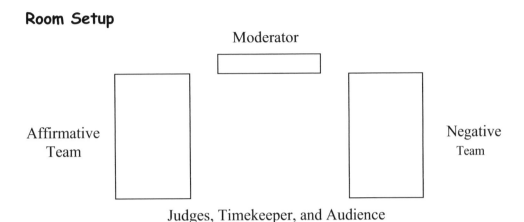

Moderator

Affirmative
Team

Negative
Team

Judges, Timekeeper, and Audience

Debate Duties

There are several jobs in a debate. The affirmative team consists of four students who support the topic (or resolution). The negative team also has four members and argues against the resolution.

The moderator keeps the debate moving by directing who will speak next. The timekeeper keeps the time of each speaker and signals the moderator when a person's time is up.

The judges judge the debate based on the arguments presented by both sides. The judges decide which side wins the debate.

Debate Format

Opening Statements – 2 minutes for each team

There are four speakers for each team. The first speaker on each team makes an opening statement. This statement tells the resolution and the main argument of the team. For example, if the resolution is wearing school uniforms, the affirmative team's statement would say it supports wearing uniforms to school and the negative team's statement would be against wearing school uniforms.

Second and Third Speakers – 2 minutes for each team

The second and third speakers from each side ask and answer questions during this part of the debate. The affirmative team questions the negative team for 2 minutes and vice versa. Both teams answer the questions the best way they can.

Planning Final Statement – 3 minutes

Members of each team talk among themselves about the debate so far and plan a closing statement to be delivered by the fourth speaker.

Fourth Speaker – 1 minute each
Fourth speakers for each team deliver closing statements summarizing their main arguments.

Judges' Decision – 3 minutes
The judges meet and discuss the debate. They rate each speaker, decide which team won the debate, then announce the winner.

Sample Judge's Sheet

Rate speakers on a scale of 1 to 4, with 4 being the best.

Affirmative Team
Speaker 1
Did the speaker present the opening statement clearly?
1   2   3   4

Did the speaker speak at a good rate?
1   2   3   4

Was the speaker convincing?
1   2   3   4

Speakers 2 and 3
Did they present questions and answers clearly?
1   2   3   4

Were they convincing?
1   2   3   4

Speaker 4
Was the closing argument well presented?
1   2   3   4

Did the speaker support the closing argument with facts presented during the debate?
1   2   3   4

Negative Team
Speaker 1
Did the speaker present the opening statement clearly?
1   2   3   4

Did the speaker speak at a good rate?
1   2   3   4

Was the speaker convincing?
1   2   3   4

Speakers 2 and 3
Did they present questions and answers clearly?
1   2   3   4

Were they convincing?
1   2   3   4

Speaker 4
Was the closing argument well presented?
1   2   3   4

Did the speaker support the closing argument with facts presented during the debate?
1   2   3   4

Attachment 11   Generalizations Rubric

Student or Team: _____

Assignment: _____

Directions: Mark the appropriate rating for each criterion. Use these individual ratings to assign an overall rating for the assignment.

RATINGS	0 Working on it!	1 Novice	2 Acceptable	3 Out of the Box!
Generalizations	Unable to make a generalization with help	Began to make generalizations between ideas with help	Made simple generalizations with little help	Made complex generalizations between ideas with no help

Extended Skills to Consider:
- making generalizations between two or more disciplines
- extending to apply generalizations to other real-world problems

Comments:

Directions

Answer the following questions as you examine the flashlight. Use another piece of paper for your answers.

1. Write down your predictions of what will be inside the flashlight. Draw a picture of what you think the inside of the flashlight will look like.

2. Write a short explanation of how you think the flashlight works.

3. Disassemble the flashlight. Draw a picture and label each part of the flashlight.

4. Write about each part of the flashlight. Determine the function of each part of the flashlight.

5. Are there any improvements you could make to this flashlight to make it better? If so, describe them.

6. Are there any parts of the flashlight that are unnecessary? If so, tell why and describe how the flashlight would function without them.

7. What purpose does the shiny area around the bulb serve?

8. Write a paragraph telling what you learned by taking apart the flashlight.

Directions

1. Gather one piece of the holiday light string, one piece of duct tape, and a 9-volt battery.

2. Use duct tape to secure one end of the wire to one terminal on the 9-volt battery.

3. Touch the loose wire to the other terminal of the battery. The bulb should light. If it does not light, be sure the duct tape is securely holding the other end of the wire on the other terminal.

4. Draw a picture of your completed circuit below. Be sure to label all the parts.

Questions
Vocabulary and Materials Checklist

Activity	Vocabulary	Materials Needed
1		5 large sheets of chart paper
2	iambic pentameter peasants playwright prevalent Renaissance	copies of Attachment 1 computer with Internet access
3	lighthearted mutt	multiple matching copies of *Because of Winn-Dixie* book, by Kate DiCamillo (at least 1 copy per two students) chart paper
4	executed hypotheses philosopher reconsider scientific method Socratic Questions	computer with Internet access
5	articles sections	old newspaper (enough for one copy per two students), highlighters
6	improvisation spontaneous	copies of Attachment 8
7	compose rhyme	assortment of poetry books science books computer with Internet access
8	evaluate	
9	modify strategies	
10	average relevant specified tally	dry erase board and marker
11	approval museum	computer with Internet access one or several of the following books: *Mistakes That Worked* by Charlotte Foltz Jones *Brainstorm!: The Stories of Twenty American Kid Inventors* by Tom Tucker *Accidents May Happen: 50 Inventions Discovered by Mistake* by Charlotte Fultz Jones *The Kid Who Invented the Popsicle: And Other Surprising Stories About Inventions* by Don L. Wulffson

12	bioluminescence Marianas Trench pressure twilight zone	*Fountains of Life: The Story of Deep-Sea Vents* book, by Elizabeth Tayntor Gowell *Slippery, Splendid Sea Creatures* book, by Madelyn Wood Carlisle computer with Internet access other books, videos, or audiotapes about life at the bottom of the ocean
13	demolish environment excursions larvae	1 package of 3 x 5 index cards sticky notes copies of Attachment 10
14	comforts harnessed technological	computer with Internet access books about inventions
15	circuit conductor discovery innovation invention	several simple items for students to disassemble and reassemble (3 flashlights, spring-loaded ball point pen, mechanical pencil) working string of holiday lights (6) 9-volt batteries 6 pieces of duct tape wire strippers wire cutters copies of Attachments 12 and 13
16	persuasive pose premise	3 bells resources about the history of your school and school district – videotapes, audiotapes, people to interview, records from the school districts, etc.
17	ancestors century descendants perspectives	several sheets of chart paper
18		5 large sheets of chart paper

Note: Paper and pencils should be on hand each day, as should writing and illustration supplies, and may not be listed on the checklist.

Questions
Differentiation Strategies and TEKS Checklist

Activity	Differentiation Strategies	TEKS: Language Arts and Reading	TEKS: Mathematics	TEKS: Social Studies	TEKS: Science
1	**Analysis and Synthesis** Critical Thinking **Multiple Perspectives** Brainstorming Point of View	Connect his/her own experiences, information, insights, and ideas with those of others through speaking and listening			
2	**Knowledge and Skills** Etymology **Analysis and Synthesis** Creative Problem Solving Evaluation	Read classic and contemporary works Read for varied purposes such as to be informed, to be entertained, to appreciate the writer's craft, and to discover models for his/her own writing			
	Ethics/Unanswered Questions Tolerance for Ambiguity Aesthetic Thinking	Establish and adjust purposes for reading such as reading to find out, to understand, to interpret, to enjoy, and to solve problems			
	Communication Writing Skills	Determine a text's main (or major) ideas and how those ideas are supported with details			

Activity	Differentiation Strategies	TEKS: Language Arts and Reading	TEKS: Mathematics	TEKS: Social Studies	TEKS: Science
		Write to express, discover, record, develop, reflect on ideas, and to problem solve Connect his/her own experiences, information, insights, and ideas with those of others through speaking and listening			Identify patterns of change such as in weather, metamorphosis, and objects in the sky
3	**Knowledge and Skills** Attributes Visualization **Multiple Perspectives** Brainstorming Point of View **Methodology and Use of Resources** Research **Communication** Writing Skills	Determine a text's main (or major) ideas and how those ideas are supported with details Paraphrase and summarize text to recall, inform, and organize ideas Write to entertain such as to compose humorous poems or short stories Use multiple sources, including electronic texts, experts, and print resources, to locate information relevant to research questions Offer observations, make connections, react, speculate, interpret, and raise questions in response to texts	Use place value to read, write, compare, and order decimals involving tenths and hundredths, including money, using concrete models Add and subtract decimals to the hundredths place using concrete and pictorial models	Translate geographic data into a variety of formats such as raw data to graphs and maps	Analyze and interpret information to construct reasonable explanations from direct and indirect evidence Represent the natural world using models and identify their limitations
4	**Knowledge and Skills**	Connect his/her own experiences, information,			

Activity	Differentiation Strategies	TEKS: Language Arts and Reading	TEKS: Mathematics	TEKS: Social Studies	TEKS: Science
	Attributes Categorizing **Analysis and Synthesis** Convergent and Divergent Thinking Creative Problem Solving **Ethics/Unanswered Questions** Provocative Questions	insights, and ideas with those of others through speaking and listening Write to express, discover, record, develop, reflect on ideas, and to problem solve Use multiple sources, including electronic texts, experts, and print resources, to locate information relevant to research questions Draw conclusions from information gathered from multiple sources Select, organize, or produce visuals to complement and extend meanings			
5	**Analysis and Synthesis** Evaluation Draw Conclusions **Multiple Perspectives** Inquiry Point of View **Communication** Writing Skills	Connect his/her own experiences, information, insights, and ideas with those of others through speaking and listening Write to express, discover, record, develop, reflect on ideas, and to problem solve Use multiple sources including electronic texts,			

Activity	Differentiation Strategies	TEKS: Language Arts and Reading	TEKS: Mathematics	TEKS: Social Studies	TEKS: Science
	Relevance and Significance Resource Person	experts, and print resources, to locate information relevant to research questions Draw conclusions from information gathered from multiple sources Select, organize, or produce visuals to complement and extend meaning			

73

Activity	Differentiation Strategies	TEKS: Language Arts and Reading	TEKS: Mathematics	TEKS: Social Studies	TEKS: Science
5		Write to inform such as to explain, describe, report, and narrate			
		Paraphrase and summarize text to recall, inform, and organize ideas			
		Demonstrate effective communications skills that reflect such demands ad interviewing, reporting, requesting, and providing information			
		Edit drafts for specific purposes such as to ensure standard usage, varied sentence structure, and appropriate word choice			
		Produce communications using technology or appropriate media such as developing a class newspaper, multimedia reports, or video reports			
6	Analysis and Synthesis Creative Problem Solving Critical Thinking Multiple	Identify the purposes of different types of texts such as to inform, influence, express, or entertain Write to entertain such as to compose humorous poems or			

74

Activity	Differentiation Strategies	TEKS: Language Arts and Reading	TEKS: Mathematics	TEKS: Social Studies	TEKS: Science
	Perspectives Brainstorming **Relevance and Significance** Role Playing	short stories Present dramatic interpretations of experiences, stories, poems, or plays to communicate Generate ideas and plans for writing by using such prewriting strategies as brainstorming, graphic organizers, notes, and logs			
7	**Knowledge and Skills** Attributes Visualization **Analysis and Synthesis** Creative Problem Solving Aesthetic Thinking **Multiple Perspectives** Brainstorming **Communication** Writing Skills	Read aloud in selected texts in ways that both reflect understanding of the text and engage the listeners Write to express, discover, record, develop, reflect on ideas, and to problem solve Form and revise questions for investigations, including questions arising from interests and units of study			

Activity	Differentiation Strategies	TEKS: Language Arts and Reading	TEKS: Mathematics	TEKS: Social Studies	TEKS: Science
8	**Knowledge and Skills** Attributes Categorizing **Analysis and Synthesis** Critical Thinking Convergent and Divergent Thinking **Multiple Perspectives** Brainstorming **Methodology and Use of Resources** Research Shares Inquiry	Write to express, discover, record develop, reflect on ideas, and to problem solve Form and revise questions for investigations, including questions arising from interests and units of study Respond in constructive ways to others' writings	Use a problem-solving model that incorporates understanding the problem, making a plan, carrying out the plan, and evaluate the solution for reasonableness	Identify different points of view about an issue or topic	
9	**Knowledge and Skills** Attributes Categorizing **Demonstration** Analysis and Synthesis Creative Problem Solving **Ethics/Unanswered Questions** Provocative Questions	Determine a purpose for listening such as to gain information, to solve problems, or to enjoy and appreciate Connect his/her own experiences, information, insights, and ideas with those of others through speaking and listening Choose the appropriate form for his/her own purpose for writing, including journals,			

76

Activity	Differentiation Strategies	TEKS: Language Arts and Reading	TEKS: Mathematics	TEKS: Social Studies	TEKS: Science
		letters, reviews, poems, narratives, and instructions Give precise directions and instructions such as in games and tasks			
10	**Knowledge and Skills** Attributes Demonstration **Analysis and Synthesis** Creative Problem Solving Critical Thinking **Communication** Decision-making	Determine a purpose for listening such as to gain information, to solve problems, or to enjoy and appreciate Connect his/her own experiences, information	Use a problem-solving model that incorporates understanding the problem, making a plan, carrying out the plan, and evaluate the solution for reasonableness Graph a given set of data using as appropriate graphical representation such as a picture or line Use addition and subtraction to solve problems involving whole numbers and decimals Use division to solve problems involving whole numbers		
11	**Knowledge and Skills** Demonstration Classifying **Analysis and Synthesis** Evaluation Generalizations	Use multiple sources, including electronic texts, experts, and print resources, to locate information relevant to research questions Establish and adjust purposes for reading such as to find out, to understand, to		Identify famous inventors and scientists such as Gail Borden, Joseph Glidden, and Patillo Higgins, and their contributions Describe how scientific discoveries and technological innovations	Evaluate the impact of research on scientific thought, society, and the environment

77

Activity	Differentiation Strategies	TEKS: Language Arts and Reading	TEKS: Mathematics	TEKS: Social Studies	TEKS: Science
	Multiple Perspectives Brainstorming	interpret, to enjoy, and to solve problems		have benefited individuals have benefited individuals, businesses, and society in Texas	
		Write to express, discover, record, develop, reflect on ideas, and to problem solve			
	Communication Research	Select, organize, or produce visuals to complement and extend meanings			
		Connect his/her own experiences, information, insights, and ideas with those of others through speaking and listening			

Activity	Differentiation Strategies	TEKS: Language Arts and Reading	TEKS: Mathematics	TEKS: Social Studies	TEKS: Science
12	**Knowledge and Skills** Research Visualization **Communication** Demonstration **Relevance and Significance** Resource Person	Connect his/her own experiences, information, insights, and ideas with those of others through speaking and listening Use multiple sources, including electronic texts, experts, and print resources, to locate information relevant to research questions Write to inform such as to explain, describe, report, and narrate Take notes from relevant and authoritative sources such as guest speakers, periodicals, and on-line searches Produce communications using technology or appropriate media such as developing a class newspaper, multimedia reports, or video reports			Analyze and describe adaptive characteristics that result in an organism's unique niche in an ecosystem Represent the natural world using models and identify their limitations

Activity	Differentiation Strategies	TEKS: Language Arts and Reading	TEKS: Mathematics	TEKS: Social Studies	TEKS: Science
13	**Knowledge and Skills** Attributes	Write to express, discover, record, develop, reflect on ideas, and to problem solve		Analyze information by sequencing categorizing, identifying cause-and-effect relationships, comparing, contrasting, finding the main idea, summarizing, making generalizations and predictions, and drawing inferences and conclusions	
	Analysis and Synthesis Creative Problem Solving	Connect his/her own experiences, information, insights, and ideas with those of others through speaking and listening			
	Multiple Perspectives Paradoxes Group Consensus	Collaborate with other writers to compose, organize, and revise various types of texts, including letters, news, records, and forms		Identify different points of view about a topic	
	Communication Decision Making	Respond in constructive ways to others' writing		Express Ideas orally based on research and experiences	

80

Activity	Differentiation Strategies	TEKS: Language Arts and Reading	TEKS: Mathematics	TEKS: Social Studies	TEKS: Science
	Analysis and Synthesis Creative Problem Solving Trend Extrapolation	Organize prior knowledge about a topic in a variety of ways such as by producing a graphic organizer		Identify famous inventors and scientists such as Gail Borden, Joseph Glidden, and Patillo Higgins, and their contributions	Evaluate the impact of research on scientific thought, society, and the environment
	Ethics/Unanswered Questions Provocative Questions Tolerance for Ambiguity	Understand the major ideas and supporting evidence in spoken messages Collaborate with other writers to compose, organize, and revise various types of texts, including letters, news, records, and forms		Describe how scientific discoveries and technological innovations have benefited individuals, businesses, and society in Texas	
14	**Multiple Perspectives** Brainstorming	Connect his/her own experiences, information, insights, and ideas with those of others through speaking and listening Use multiple sources, including electronic texts, experts, and print resources, to locate information relevant to research questions Write to inform such as to explain, describe, report, and narrate			

Activity	Differentiation Strategies	TEKS: Language Arts and Reading	TEKS: Mathematics	TEKS: Social Studies	TEKS: Science
15	**Knowledge and Skills** Attributes Visualization **Analysis and Synthesis** Analogies Evaluation Creative Thinking **Multiple Perspectives** Brainstorming	Establish and adjust purposes for reading such as reading to find out, to understand, to interpret, to enjoy, and to solve problems Determine the purposes for listening such as to gain information, to solve problems, or to enjoy and appreciate Connect his/her own experiences, information, insights, and ideas with those of others through speaking and listening		Communicate in written, oral, and visual forms Write to inform such as to explain, describe, report, and narrate Use problem-solving and decision making skills Identify different points of view about an issue or topic	Plan and implement descriptive investigations including asking well-defined questions, formulating testable hypotheses, and selecting and using equipment and technology Analyze and interpret information to construct reasonable explanations from direct and indirect evidence Represent the natural world using models and identify their limitations

82

Activity	Differentiation Strategies	TEKS: Language Arts and Reading	TEKS: Mathematics	TEKS: Social Studies	TEKS: Science
16	**Knowledge and Skills** Research **Multiple Perspectives** Shared Inquiry Brainstorming **Relevance and Significance** Resource Persons	Connect his/her own experiences, information, insights, and ideas with those of others through speaking and listening Use multiple sources, including electronic texts, experts, and print resources, to locate information relevant to research questions Collaborate with other writers to compose, organize, and revise various types of texts, including letters, news, records, and forms Frame questions to direct research			
17	**Analysis and Synthesis** Draw Conclusions Creative Problem Solving Trend Extrapolation **Multiple Perspectives** Brainstorming **Communication** Writing Skills	Connect his/her own experiences, information, insights, and ideas with those of others through speaking and listening Frame questions to direct research Write to express, discover, record, develop, reflect on ideas, and to problem solve		Express ideas orally based on research and experiences Identify different points of view about an issue or topic	

83

Activity	Differentiation Strategies	TEKS: Language Arts and Reading	TEKS: Mathematics	TEKS: Social Studies	TEKS: Science
18	**Analysis and Synthesis** Critical Thinking **Multiple Perspectives** Brainstorming	Connect his/her own experiences, information, insights, and ideas with those of others through speaking and listening			

Questions
National Standards Checklist

Activity	Language Arts and Reading	Mathematics	Social Studies	Science
1	Uses prewriting strategies to plan written work Uses prior knowledge and experience to understand and respond to new information Contributes to group discussions			
2	Writes narrative accounts, such as poems and stories Writes in response to literature Uses electronic media to gather information Reads aloud familiar stories, poems, and passages with fluency and expression Establishes purpose for reading	Recognizes a wide variety of patterns and the rules that explain them	History Understands calendar time in years, decades, and centuries Understands that specific individuals had a great impact on history Evaluates historical fiction according to the accuracy of its content and the author's interpretation	
3	Writes expository composition Writes narrative accounts, such as poems and stories Writes in response to literature	Solves real-world problems involving number operations Understands the basic measures perimeter, area, volume, capacity, mass, angle, and circumference	Geography Knows major physical and human features of places as they are represented on maps and globes Understands how stories, legends,	Knows that the patterns of stars in the sky stay the same, although they appear to slowly move from east to west across the sky nightly and different stars can be seen in different seasons

Activity	Language Arts and Reading	Mathematics	Social Studies	Science
	Writes personal letters		songs, ballads, games, and tall tales describe the environment, lifestyles, beliefs, and struggles of people in various regions of the country	Knows that planets look like stars, but over time they appear to wander among the constellations
	Makes, confirms, and revises simple predictions about what will be found in a text			
	Understands the author's purpose			
	Understands elements of character development in literary works			
	Makes inferences or Draw Conclusions about characters' qualities and actions			
	Makes connections between characters or simple events in a literary work and people or events in his or her own life			
	Contributes to group discussions			
4	Uses strategies to draft and revise written work	Understands that data represent specific pieces of information about real-world objects or activities	History Understands calendar time in years, decades, and centuries	Knows that scientists review and ask questions about the results of other scientists' work
	Uses a variety of strategies to plan research		Understands that specific individuals had a great impact on history	Knows that scientific investigations involve asking and answering a question and comparing the answer to what scientists already know about the world
	Uses electronic media to gather information	Organizes and displays data in simple bar graphs, pie charts, and line graphs	Understands that specific ideas had an impact on history	
	Responds to questions and	Recognizes events that are sure to		

Activity	Language Arts and Reading	Mathematics	Social Studies	Science
	comments Makes basic oral presentations to class	happen, events that are sure not to happen, and events that may or may not happen		Knows that people of all ages, backgrounds, and groups have made contributions to science and technology throughout history
5	Uses strategies to edit and publish written work Evaluates own and others' writing Uses strategies to write for different audiences Uses strategies to write for a variety of purposes Uses a variety of strategies to plan research Uses strategies to compile information into written reports or summaries			
6	Uses strategies to write for different audiences Uses strategies to write for a variety of purposes Asks questions in class Makes basic oral presentations to class			

Activity	Language Arts and Reading	Mathematics	Social Studies	Science
7	Uses a variety of verbal communication skills Writes narrative accounts, such as poems and stories Writes expressive compositions Uses a variety of strategies to plan research Uses electronic media to gather information			Knows that scientists use different kinds of investigations depending on the questions they are trying to answer
8	Evaluates own and others' writing Uses a variety of strategies to plan research Uses prior knowledge and experience to understand and respond to new information	Uses a variety of strategies to understand problem situations Uses trial and error and the process of elimination to solve problems		
9	Uses a variety of strategies to plan research Uses prior knowledge and experience to understand and respond to new information Listens to classmates and adults Uses strategies to convey a clear main point when speaking		Knows the characteristics of an effective rule or law	
10	Uses strategies to write for a variety of purposes	Knows the difference between pertinent and irrelevant		

Activity	Language Arts and Reading	Mathematics	Social Studies	Science
	Uses multiple representations of information to find information for research topics Uses prior knowledge and experience to understand and respond to new information Contributes to group discussions Responds to questions and comments Listens to classmates and adults	information when solving problems Understands basic number theory concepts Understands the basic difference between odd and even numbers Understands the basic meaning of place value Adds, subtracts, multiplies, and divides whole numbers and decimal Understands that spreading data out on a number line helps to see what the extremes are, where the data points pile up, and where the gaps are Organizes and displays data in simple bar graphs, pie charts, and line graphs		
11	Uses prewriting strategies to plan written work Writes narrative accounts, such as poems and stories Uses a variety of strategies to plan research		Economics Knows that innovation is the introduction of an invention into a use that has economic value Knows that entrepreneurs are people who use resources to produce innovative goods and services they hope people will buy	Plans and conducts simple investigations Knows that people of all ages, backgrounds, and groups have made contributions to science and technology throughout history Knows that although people using

Activity	Language Arts and Reading	Mathematics	Social Studies	Science
	Uses electronic media to gather information		History Understands that specific individuals had a great impact on history	scientific inquiry have learned much about the objects, events, and phenomena in nature, science is an ongoing process and will never be finished
	Uses strategies to compile information into written reports or summaries		Understands that specific ideas had an impact on history	Knows that scientists and engineers often work in teams to accomplish a task
	Establishes purpose for reading		Understands that "chance events" had an impact on history	
	Uses reading skills and strategies to understand a variety of informational texts		Knows about technological inventions and developments that evolved during the 19th century and the influence of these changes on the lives of workers	
	Responds to questions and comments		Knows the significant scientific and technological achievements of various historical societies	
	Organizes ideas for oral presentations			

90

Activity	Language Arts and Reading	Mathematics	Social Studies	Science
12	Writes expository compositions Uses a variety of strategies to plan research Uses electronic media to gather information Uses strategies to compile information into written reports or summaries Organizes ideas for oral presentations			Knows that plants and animals progress through life cycles of birth, growth and development, reproduction, and death; the details of these life cycles are different for different organisms Knows that living organisms have distinct structures and body systems that serve specific functions in growth, survival, and reproduction Knows that an organism's patterns of behavior are related to the nature of that organism's environment

91 © Prufrock Press Inc.

Activity	Language Arts and Reading	Mathematics	Social Studies	Science
13	Writes expository compositions Uses a variety of strategies to plan research Uses electronic media to gather information Makes basic oral presentations to class	Solves real-world problems involving number operations Understands the basic concept of a sample Recognizes events that are sure to happen, events that are sure not to happen, and events that may or may not happen Understands that numbers and the operations performed on them can be used to describe things in the real world and predict what might occur	Economics Knows that innovation is the introduction of an invention into a use that has economic value History Understands that specific individuals had a great impact of history Understands the influence of Enlightenment ideas on American society	Knows the organization of a simple electrical circuit Knows that people of all ages, backgrounds, and groups have made contributions to science and technology throughout history Knows that although people using scientific inquiry have learned much about the objects, events, and phenomena in nature, science is an ongoing process and will never be finished Knows that scientists and engineers often work in teams to accomplish a task

Activity	Language Arts and Reading	Mathematics	Social Studies	Science
14	Writes expository compositions Uses a variety of strategies to plan research Uses electronic media to gather information Makes basic oral presentations to class		Economics Knows that innovation is the introduction of an invention into a use that has economic value History Understands that specific individuals had a great impact on history Understands the influence of Enlightenment ideas on American society	Knows the organization of a simple electrical circuit Knows that people of all ages, backgrounds, and groups have made contributions to science and technology throughout history Knows that although people using scientific inquiry have learned much about the objects, events, and phenomena in nature, science is an ongoing process and will never be finished Knows that scientists and engineers often work in teams to accomplish a task

Activity	Language Arts and Reading	Mathematics	Social Studies	Science
15	Uses prewriting strategies to plan written work Uses paragraph form in writing Uses a variety of strategies to plan research	Uses basic sample spaces to describe and predict events	Economics Knows that innovation is the introduction of an invention into a use that has economic value History Understands that specific individuals had a great impact of history Knows about the development of the wheel and its early uses in ancient societies Understands the development and the influence of basic tools on work and behavior Understands the influence of Enlightenment ideas on American society	Knows the organization of a simple electrical circuit Knows that people of all ages, backgrounds, and groups have made contributions to science and technology throughout history Knows that although people using scientific inquiry have learned much about the objects, events, and phenomena in nature, science is an ongoing process and will never be finished Knows that scientists and engineers often work in teams to accomplish a task

94

Activity	Language Arts and Reading	Mathematics	Social Studies	Science
16	Uses strategies to write for a variety of purposes Uses a variety of strategies to plan research Uses electronic media to gather information Uses strategies to gather and record information for research topics Uses strategies to compile information into written reports or summaries			
17	Uses a variety of strategies to plan research Contributes to group discussions		History Understands calendar time in years, decades, and centuries Distinguishes between past, present, and future time	Knows that people of all ages, backgrounds, and groups have made contributions to science and technology throughout history Knows that although people using scientific inquiry have learned much about the objects, events, and phenomena in nature, science is an ongoing process and will never be finished
18	Uses prewriting strategies to plan written work Uses prior knowledge and experience to understand and respond to new information			